Writing My Dictionary

poems by

Dennis Herrell

Finishing Line Press
Georgetown, Kentucky

Writing My Dictionary

Copyright © 2017 by Dennis Herrell
ISBN 978-1-63534-133-1 First Edition
All rights reserved under International and Pan-American Copyright Conventions. No part of this book may be reproduced in any manner whatsoever without written permission from the publisher, except in the case of brief quotations embodied in critical articles and reviews.

ACKNOWLEDGMENTS

Acknowledgments of previously published poems

Afternoon Poem	by *un-Aurorean*
Gracias Senor Marquez	by *Abbey*
Knowing Wonder	by *Pegasus*
Lust in the Air	by *Pennine Ink*
All the Marbles	by *Mid-America Poetry Review*
No Roses	by *Parnassus Literary Journal*
Reading Your Poetry	by *Pegasus*
Transformation	by *Maelstrom*
X-ray	by *Poem*
Younger Days	by *Abbey*

Publisher: Leah Maines

Editor: Christen Kincaid

Cover Art: https://pixabay.com/en/old-retro-antique-vintage-classic-1130743/

Author Photo: Dennis Herrell

Cover Design: Elizabeth Maines

Printed in the USA on acid-free paper.
Order online: www.finishinglinepress.com
　　　　　also available on amazon.com

Author inquiries and mail orders:
Finishing Line Press
P. O. Box 1626
Georgetown, Kentucky 40324
U. S. A.

Table of Contents

Afternoon Poem 1
Bodies 101 2
Celebrations 3
Day Trading 4
Each 5
Forecast 6
Gracias, Senor Marquez 7
How I Sinned on Tuesday 8
Inside 9
Junior Year 10
Knowing Wonder 11
Lust in the Air 12
Marbles 13
No Roses 14
Or Else 15
Putting Yourself in a Room 16
Questions 17
Reading Your Poetry 18
Small Essentials 19
Transformation 20
UP 21
Venus de Me 22
Waiting 23
X-ray 24
Younger Days 25
Zen at the Checkout 26

A   Afternoon Poem

The poem hung like a strange fruit on the monitor,
as if uncertain about its ripeness
and how easily available it should be to a stranger.

The writer walked past it for a kitchen glass of water. On the way back
he paused for a moment of study. He drank water and gurgled,
thought about the purification of his body, how it might affect the poem.

He leaned over the keyboard,
moved the curser to the left,
deleted 'a' and put 'the' in its place.

The writer had changed the articles of war in that decisive moment.
The chess game of poetry had quickened with a new sense of urgency.
But he must pace himself. It would be a long afternoon with this triangle
of love

between him,
the computer,
and the poem.

B   Bodies 101

Our bodies have their way with us,
have done so over millenniums -
arms quite selectively
do what they think is best, reaching
for things right in the fire.
Legs find cliffs and gopher holes.
Ears hear mosquitoes and ignore
the lions outside our tents of sleep.
Colons care only for their little coiled
worlds of digestion and disorder.

Eyes see cosmetics and fold of fabric,
give no notice to avarice or deceit.
Hearts speak of love but murmur
lies about life and state of health.
Our bodies busy themselves with bad breath,
sweaty armpits, funky crotches,
and noses dripping mucus - all too much
for our rational minds, so occupied
with placating demanding egos
in a world of mirrors.

C   **Celebrations**

And he got the box labeled Beach House.
Contents: Blue Willow plates & saucers
wrapped in the daily news;
also 3 Bama water glasses,
which rather limited his dinner parties
unless someone agreed not to be thirsty.

However, he thought he would keep all this
for special occasions -
like the anniversary of her varicose veins,
the festivities of their last fight,
the ceremonies of separation
            and divorce,

and the
hitherto, uncelebrated anniversary of the collapse
of the American family unit.

D   Day Trading

Once was enough on that day.
I would not ask for more.
No one was noticing
my bubbles of delight rising to the surface,
no one hearing that wild cry captured in the chest.

One look around the room bought me sensibility.
There were my shoes piled in the corner,
a chair had collected three days of clothes and a sad towel,
curser blinked on waiting mode.
I should not ask for more.

E   Each

Each man involved
in his maelstrom of desire
confronts a riddled world,

cannot evolve beyond
the contrary belief that what is
shouldn't be what controls him.

Less than more
cannot be enough for a man
concerned about the nature of things.

What happens when the big question
collides with the bang of universe
to form so many light years of waiting?

Can he find one small bit of matter after that?

F   Forecast

The weather is fair
but subject to change.
My health is on the meter
with time running out
and me without quarters.
Healthcare doesn't care
because congress doesn't need it
and is too busy with reelection.
Social security is a bare
cupboard hoarding rusting
cans of spinach and applesauce,
and is growing older by the minute.
The market is a yo-yo
on a time-frayed string
with hedge funds
walking the dog
and doing loop the loops around the world.
Bankers are playing cards with our money
with aces in the hole
and keeping all the winnings.
Education is in a class by itself
with every principal and principle
failing in the back of the room.
So the weather is fair but mostly cloudy
with warnings in the air,
and like my blood pressure
very subject to change.

G   Gracias, Senor Marquez

Gabriel Garcia Marquez
has a gypsy say   things have a life of their own
which even now helps explain
why you can't find your keys
because actually
the keys have by themselves become lost,

or perhaps in mischief
are off hiding in a secret place,
and in M's book   *One Hundred Years of Solitude*
                        (while looking for everything)
the gypsy will sell you believably magical magnets
to ease your troubled search.

All this I learned in the first two pages
and did not need to read any further
in this fine informational book that
although written by a foreigner
all the words were in English,
which made it easy for me to understand
the complicated and international issues of lost keys.

H   How I Sinned on Tuesday

Forgive me, Father,
for I have sinned once more.
When the clerk of innocence
at Epicurean
questioned with confused eye and tone,
I answered without hesitation,
green beans,
instead of righteous
and expensive, sugar snaps,
and walked away with wrongful excess.

I   Inside

He was standing in the doorway
watching stillness,
watching for movement,
too cautious
to enter the outside
without more thought about consequences,
how one action led to another,
then once more another,
till he was deep in the bother of things:

how friends died faster
than babies renewing,
how jobs required his hands
to restore order;
the old Chevy waited for destinations
that didn't matter because he needed less now,
wouldn't last longer than worn clothes,
and he didn't want to go up a hill to look down.
He could see it all from his door.

J Junior Year

The young women
we said girls
names like Toni, Sandra, Betty Ann
wore clothes that made their bodies invisible
skirts down to their ankles
so they moved with steps so short
their breasts
we called them tits
didn't bounce beneath barely seen bra straps
and hidden anyway by armfuls of books
we had never read but volunteered to carry
and girl parts we knew to be asses
only slightly quivered under maiden fabric
but we were hot-blooded enough to know
there were things there that we wanted
and we stammered, stuttered and stalled
as we stood before the actual live creations
of last night's creamy dreams on hot tossed beds.

K   Knowing Wonder

You walked over mountains
and put clouds under your feet,
watched evening pull down the shades,
saw stars overcoming a black night.

You heard the leaves
grow with subtle chlorophyll,
divining a way through a subway
not as deep as a circuit board.

You saw many flowers,
some in the guise of women,
but those with more than a mortal grace
lingered longer.

You heard birdsong
stronger in the hills, and happier,
than the canned laughter
from a thin television in a thin room.

L   Lust in the Air

He pleaded ignorance, then a malady,
but the evening had still ended
with a hot discussion
in the cool air
with cross-pollination happening

madly about them, microspores everywhere,
pollen clouds erupting from sexy pollenizers,
free love pollinators sweet-talking young stigmas
into lowering their pistil guards
for just one moment of midnight bliss.

He sneezed and wheezed his red-eyed way
down the garden path to home.

M   Marbles

First,
scrape a circle in the dirt,
about six feet across,
and do it with a stick.

Second,
check and count your marbles,
choose your best shooter,
feel the weight of it.

Third,
start with your knuckles in the dirt
and on the line,
shoot straight and hard and true.

This is not a kid's game.
This is for all the marbles.

N   No Roses

Spain is no longer where I want to go.
No matter how many times
I see the bullfight,
Hemingway will not be there
telling me the clean truth.

Italy basks in the sun within cities
ancestered by empire and city-states.
Holy papal dictum, a splash of renaissance,
and a dose of Mussolini all resulted in
a social mix I study over pasta and wine.

Paris in the spring
has the art but not the flair
of Gertrude Stein holding court
among the roses.

London will be misty and green,
full of soft light,
but without the clarity
of T.S. Eliot to let me hear
how people speak,

and watch the way they walk
toward the end of the long English line.
I will not go anywhere
to find so much gone.

O   Or Else

She never directly says it
but my girlfriend cajoles
and thereby suggests in her way
that minor dinner mishaps
and/or the withholding of sex
might somehow occur
if I don't agree to join her
in the unmanly watching
of genetically engineered
sentimental stories like
White Christmas
Emma
Downton Abbey
Miracle on 34th Street
Jane Eyre
It's a Wonderful Life
Sense and Sensibility
Holiday Inn
I will enjoy them she implies,
Or else.

P   Putting Yourself in a Room

Having art on the wall is like
relaxing in your room
while visiting with friends:

Taking a walk together through a landscape,
nodding with the trees, kneeling in the grass,
dreaming about your common mountain.

A still-life arrangement made by familiar hands,
each piece admired for shape and texture,
uncensored for its color.

An abstract or impressionism that fits in nicely
with your kaleidoscopic mind,
creating more vivid images in your inner movie.

A portrait of someone you knew by name
but now everyday becomes a fellow spirit,
freed from a set place in time.

You can take a walk around your room, then be
elsewhere, enriched within the artistic realm
of friends   scenes   impressions   memories.

Q   Questions

After I murdered the fly
I asked myself
why
why could I not live
with the innocent
buzz of nature?

After I pinned the butterfly
I asked myself
why
why did I have to own
that rare display
of living color?

After I plucked the daisy
I asked myself
why
why would I exchange
that wonder nodding in the wind
for a dying flower in my hand?

After I constrained
the laughing child
I asked myself
why
why would I wish to live
in a silent world?

R   Reading Your Poetry

I have never seen you
met your face
felt a firm hand on my arm
heard voice from actual mouth.

I know only your images
pebbled moments rippling
ideas giving multiple birth
descriptions making mud into walls.

You might be
Mr.   Mrs.   Ms.
young   old   or
middle-aged bartender.

I don't care.

I got jolted awake
by your crazy
faraway idea for a poem.
That's good enough for me.

S   Small Essentials

I want to see with the eyes
that see the way of the Haiku

eyes that can recognize
the small essence of a small essential

the eyes of Buddha's humility
looking out over the human landscape:

the social truths of a committee meeting
bored eyes, pencil tapping, doodles, yawns

the details of a dragonfly's wing
only if you desire to look

the initial flicker of doubt
when asked the unexpected question

the pattern of rocks on a difficult trail
you follow because you have to

the bond between mother and child
because of a giving nipple

the glimpse of moon
behind the starkness of outlined tree

the moon, the tree, the night, and a small me.

T   Transformation

Greg
   was a
      used-to-be
         Yankee
now lives southern.

Married   Fathered
a   a new latte
southern   daughter
belle.   for old New Orleans.

Greg
   especially
      does
         crawfish boil
bubbling boiling propane pot

mudbugs   cayenne
corn   garlic
potatoes   Zataraine's
mushrooms   file'

Make you wanta dance
and
maybe slap your mama.

U   UP

You did not have boundaries,
a horizon working with your eye
to give you sense of limit,

saying don't try to possess this far,
don't throw your power past this line
that is a sacred mark for endeavor.

You did not worry
about how far was up,
how many bodies must be stacked

as your staircase to reach the top.
It became simply a matter of logistics
and the counting of extra-spatial favors.

You were not concerned
if you were facing up or down
at any moment of social climax,

there at the peak, and you,
ready with the red flush of power,
were primed to make the next advance.

V   Venus de Me

Gillette
  (once)
    (only)
      (for)
        (men)
    Razor Company
says
    on national television
it can make me feel like a goddess,
with
  long
    tanned
      legs
        so
         s m o o t h
that I should exhibit myself on the beach.
Just curve
      my fingers around
that lovely tempting shaft
      of the Venus Razor
  (now)
    (only)
      (for)
        (women)
and I will be in another world.

W   Waiting

Casablanca
and Bogart

Bogart
and Casablanca

one a man lost
the other a city of strays

fused together in a timeless world
grown worn and wise

in a nightclub
waiting for a Bergman passing through.

X   X-ray

Nothing to fear.
Your organs
   (you know you have organs)
will never discover the intrusion.

What do they care—
too busy functioning,
sorting out the mechanics
of living,

too busy caretaking
   (you have organs for this)
for concern
about such a little growth,

such a small foreigner
in a busy system.

Y   Younger Days

You had my younger days,
that eager me teaching fresh starts
and careful language,
letting children see their own poets
being born.

You had my time of young muscles
with their frenzies, quick reflexes,
and strength to get all work done.

You had my bright eyes,
before delusion and weary tears
blurred the miracle of creating wonder -
before disenchantment.

Z   Zen at the Checkout

The moment of Zen awaits you
the very instant you enter the line
at the grocery checkout,
as this now is the time
for self-delivery into another line dimension—
an inner hum of peace and acceptance.

Dennis Herrell lives and writes in a 1920's bungalow in an old historic residential part of Houston, Texas. He writes both serious and humorous poems about his life in this civilized society. (Poking fun at himself is almost a full-time job.) He especially likes to look at the small things in everyday life that make us (him) so individual and vulnerable.

Dennis is a former teacher, a sporting goods wholesaler, a gift/card wholesaler, and then an antique dealer. He is now retired, but still actively and happily engaged in writing his poetry. Since 2001 Dennis has published about 500 poems in many U.S. journals and magazines, and about 20 poems also in Canada, Great Britain, and Austria. He has recent acceptances by *Atlanta Review, Aura, the Aurorean, Christian Science Monitor, Blue Unicorn, Iodine Poetry Journal, Pearl, Poem, Poet Lore*, and others.

Publications in other countries—*Ascent Aspiration Magazine* (CA), *Current Accounts* (UK), *Ink, Sweat, & Tears* (UK), *Ottawa Arts Review* (CA), *Pennine Ink* (UK), and *Poetry Salzburg Review* (AT).

One poetry book, *About Women*, by Book/Locker.com, 2016. Hardcover 156 pages.

www.ingramcontent.com/pod-product-compliance
Lightning Source LLC
LaVergne TN
LVHW050046090426
835510LV00043B/3326